Some Electric Hum

Some Electric Hum

Janice Northerns

LITERARY PRESS
LAMAR UNIVERSITY

ISBN: 978-1-942956-79-2
Library of Congress Control Number: 2020942733

Cover Photo: Bruno Minkley
Editor: Hannah Morris

Lamar University Literary Press
Beaumont, Texas

for Bill, partner in all things

Recent Poetry from Lamar University Literary Press

Walter Bargen, *My Other Mother's Red Mercedes*
Mark Busby, *Through Our Times*
Julie Chappell, *Mad Habits of a Life*
Stan Crawford, *Resisting Gravity*
Glover Davis, *My Cap of Darkness*
William Virgil Davis, *The Bones Poems*
Jeffrey DeLotto, *Voices Writ in Sand*
Chris Ellery, *Elder Tree*
Dede Fox, *On Wings of Silence*
Alan Gann, *That's Entertainment*
Larry Griffin, *Cedar Plums*
Michelle Hartman, *Irony and Irrelevance*
Katherine Hoerth, *Goddess Wears Cowboy Boots*
Michael Jennings, *Crossings: A Record of Travel*
Gretchen Johnson, *A Trip Through Downer, Minnesota*
Ulf Kirchdorfer, *Chewing Green Leaves*
Jim McGarrah, *A Balancing Act*
J. Pittman McGehee, *Nod of Knowing*
Laurence Musgrove, *Bluebonnet Sutras*
Benjamin Myers, *Black Sunday*
Godspower Oboido, *Wandering Feet on Pebbled Shores*
Carol Coffee Reposa, *Underground Musicians*
Jan Seale, *The Parkinson Poems*
Steven Schroeder, *the moon, not the finger, pointing*
Glen Sorestad, *Hazards of Eden*
Vincent Spina, *The Sumptuous Hills of Gulfport*
W.K. Stratton, *Ranchero Ford/ Dying in Red Dirt Country*
Wally Swist, *Invocation*
Ken Waldman, *Sports Page*
Loretta, Diane Walker, *Ode to My Mother's Voice*
Dan Williams, *Past Purgatory, a Distant Paradise*
Jonas Zdanys, *Three White Horses*

For information on these and other Lamar University Literary Press
books go to www.Lamar.edu/literarypress

Acknowledgments

Grateful acknowledgment is made to the following publications in which these poems first appeared:

Boomer Lit Magazine: "Some Electric Hum"
Borderlands: *Texas Poetry Review*: "Joseph Mans the Swings"
CCTE Studies: "Plate Tectonics"
Cabinet of Heed: "Keeping Watch as My Ex-Husband Dies"
Cagibi: "My Brothers Teach Me What It Means to Grow Up Male in West Texas"
Chariton Review: "Someone Found"
Coal City Review: "Wildcatter in a Dry County"
Cold Mountain Review: "The Promised Land" (entitled "Crossroads")
College English: "Boys Would Come on Horses"
Concho River Review: "Flying Fish," "The Playwright's Daughter," "Snake Trails," and "Zinnia Women"
Culebra!: "White Buffalo Night"
damselfly press: "Flying Off the Overpass"
descant: "Wake Up Call"
Door is Ajar Magazine: "About Those Shoes," "Last Breath," and "Driving Back from Bandolier"
Faultline: "My First Year Teaching Seventh-Grade English" and "She is a Secret"
Flint Hills Review: "Anniversary"
Gravel Magazine: "Invasive Species"
Harbinger: "Running Red Lights" (entitled "Running Stop Lights") and "Self-Composure"
Iron Horse Literary Review: "Sparks"
Jabberwock Review: "Floaters"
The Laurel Review: "Fireflies"
New Texas: "Bobbie's Valediction" and "A Texas Girl on Central Avenue"
not very quiet: "Freshman Composition" and "Hot Pink"
Poem: "Halloween, Albuquerque"
RiverSedge: "Breaking City Ordinances"

Roanoke Review: "Remembering His Name"

The Rectangle: "One July Night" (entitled "On the Night of July 22")

Santa Fe Literary Review: "North Star"

SLANT: "Opening Night"

Slush Pile Magazine: "Tornado Vision"

Smoky Blue Literary and Arts Magazine: "Mother-Daughter
Dresses"

Southwest Review: "Hammock Psalm"

Southwestern American Literature: "Break Time at El Rancho," "A
History for Louise," "Shedding," and "Tips"

Third Wednesday: "Hummingbird," "Pronoun Reference," and
"Silver Spoon"

Typishly: "Coming Out of Rough Creek Canyon"

Virtual Artists Collective: "Grandfather of the Bottomland," "The
Creative Writing Teacher Explains Love," and "Real Estate
Values"

Wraparound South: "Toss" and "Sylvia."

CONTENTS

ONE

TWO

THREE

FOUR

FIVE

ONE

White Buffalo Night

His original skin hung
on a ranch house wall, but the statue
is what everyone saw. Faded fiberglass
on a Texas courthouse lawn, the buffalo,
once white, had gone a little gray
around the edges but still marked
J. Wright Mooar's excellent hot-leaded aim.

In October, townspeople came out
for White Buffalo Days, a pageant
of cow chip pitching and stick-horse
rodeos bland enough to make them forget
they celebrated killing
the one albino who strayed
into gun range,
his pale fur the luminous beacon
in a herd of thick dark beasts.

He stood, a glass-eyed sentinel
grown manmade cold, a reminder
that people here prize what's different,
as long as it's dead. I know
the feel of feet cemented
to alien ground, breath stopped
for being the only one of your kind.

And so, first night my own feet
were loosed, I stole down
silent streets, paved black in asphalt
not meant for buffalo hoof or a girl's
bare foot, and found his aching corner
on the courthouse square.

Tenderly I broke each leg,
then soothed the wounds' sorrow
with a cool foreign tongue. And wrapped
in the robe of my woman-silk skin,
together we left this town
with every step's freed lightning
trailing a jagged glow.

Invasive Species

We unpacked in Palo Duro Canyon's
Cow Camp Cabin #3. Roughing it—
unless you count microwave, lights, noisy

window AC. We'd stopped on the way in
for firewood, park brochure warning: *Don't bring
your own: a risk of invasive species*

tagging along. We thought of forefathers
who'd invaded this place, drove Comanches
out. A cardinal dipped down to drink at the

dripping hydrant; cottontail paused as we
started up the path, waiting his turn.
Some did not concede defeat so easily.

Vultures circled each morning, waiting for
a misstep. Rat droppings in the fireplace
telegraphed their turf. Come midnight, we bolted

upright, a racket of bumps, crashes, and
clawing scratches at screen calling to mind
every tale of crazed serial killers

creeping into camp. Though the next day's search
revealed truth—just raccoons hauling corncobs
to cabin's tin roof—on that night we lay

paralyzed, as native noise, chilling
as any war whoop, drowned out the iced hum
of civilization, marking out our graves.

Toss

Always a line at this booth—toss the ring
at three-liter targets of Coke, Mr. Pibb—
keep what you rope. Three in a row nabs
the grand prize and this is what draws them in—

live rabbits. A white one, pink-eyed runt, bald
in spots and none too spunky is all that's left
tonight. The children beg anyway
for this automatic warm body. The man
in the booth downs several Coors before the whiners
arrive, sneaks a couple more into his cup

as kids cart off dusty carbonated
trophies. The air around him is a rabbit rustle
in his head. Carnival closes and he limps
back to his trailer, flipping Coors caps

as he checks the rabbit cages. Just one
dead from heat today. The dog, a Blue Heeler
heavy with ticks, knows this part of the game.
He waits, lapping empty air while the man
culls rabbit from cage, ants already fringing
its eyes. The man flicks the prize to his dog's
waiting jaws

and the rabbit tumbles through the dark
like an acrobat. Perfect toss.

Wildcatter in a Dry County

Carnival pulled out last night and glistening
greased chili dog wrappers catch the Sunday
morning light as the old man stumbles
through good times tossed on the ground.
He noses through dusty ticket stubs and Coke cups
coated in tobacco spit, thrusting the silver rod
of a metal detector before him like a hard-on
or a crutch.

The town's closed down for church; it's just him
and this rattling dowser. Each tick
speeds his heart along, though he knows bottle caps
and dimes to be the likely finds. Last month
he stirred loose a gold chain, 24 karat filigree.
No one to give it to, but the promise of a solid strike
beats faintly on in the dirt. Once his blood pumped
strong as a 30 barrel-a-day well,

back in the '50's, the oil boom. A wildcatter
could sink a few thousand into the ground
and have it come up covered in crude,
the sweet stench spicing his nights with women
and celebrity. A photo hangs in the local museum—
Bob Hope shaking his hand, smiling, partners
on twelve wells. Only one came in a gusher,
but that was enough—until the oil played out

and his woman hightailed it with a man
in Lucchese boots. Forty years later, the pump jacks
and drilling rigs have given way to churches
pumping out salvation on every corner. Members
congregate at the DQ to pick apart the sermon
as a Sunday sandstorm scours his skin. He limps back
to his rented room at the Pal-O-Mar, wipes the grime
from a few coins and his face, searching

for something worth saving. The aquifer's going dry
too, and he thinks of all that water sucked
into church baptistries—so much
to wash away the sins of the world
that he's left with not one tear
to water down the grit.

Silver Spoon

Your mother, divesting herself of history,
gave each of you a silver spoon with a story
tied round its neck: sterling heirlooms buried
beneath ancestral plantation on the eve
of Mississippi's Battle of Iuka.

I frame yours atop a fading photo
of the house: two-story columned cliché
of antebellum South. But once it hangs,
you worry that spoon into a Confederate flag,
family relic now a beacon of shining blame.

Shall we melt down silver and remake the past,
mold it into a badge of whitewashed hearts?
No, let us choose to keep it—if not on the wall,
then at least in plain sight—a heaping spoon
of gritted ash, reflecting tarnished light.

Sylvia

Sylvia was back home, grown
at sixteen, married a year
with a baby, we heard, though
all we saw of him were snapshots
of dark curls, fine solemn
eyes. *Pretty enough to be a girl, ain't he,*
Sylvia said of Little Buster, named
for his daddy.

Hospital nurses put a bow
in those dark curls, enraging
Daddy Buster, but what did that matter
when Social Services took the baby
five months later anyway?

Too much drinkin' and fightin',
Sylvia's grandma sighed.
*Too much to raise a baby
in that house.*

But the problem was not too much
of anything, I guessed,
remembering Sylvia at ten
on her grandma's porch,
bare toes stubbing dirt drab
as her hair, as she waited for her daddy
under a scalding August sun.

He finally showed, stirring dust
in a rusted black Pontiac,
smiling like he never left.
But there beside him, his latest
new wife, smoking a Lucky Strike,

the fleshy web between her thumb
and finger crudely tattooed
with some other man's initials.

Sylvia's daddy pulled a present
from the car, a Chatty Cathy doll
that talked. Only this one didn't.
Well, I found it on clearance
at the Dixie Mart, he said, *but it's still*
pretty, as pretty as . . .

And Sylvia held her breath, hoping
just for a second he might say her name.

But the new wife eyed him, said *it's time*,
and they slid back into cracked leather
seats, leaving Sylvia holding that broken bargain
doll in her arms, a little something
to call her own.

Grandfather of the Bottomland

A grainy eight-millimeter movie
is how I choose to know you,
grandfather who died when I was two. It shows
your only smile as you stand, blurry and mute,

stale cornbread in your hand,
feeding the multitudes of catfish. The fish heft
their silver weight out of a cloudy stock tank
and onto the bank for your gift, prompting that smile,
thin as the celluloid that holds it.

In all other photos you pose grim,
a stark patriarch whose children picked cotton
even on Christmas Day. Crops came first.
Visitors praised your small plot:
Fine piece of bottomland you got here, Mr. Davis.

Even this got only a silent nod.
Dry-land cotton showed nothing of a wife
dying in childbirth or the baby girl
she left behind, nothing to suckle her

but your rough knuckle. Sterling City grandparents
took her in and never gave her back,
while you raised others who came later
on grits and syrup—the ones, including my father—
who walked the fields barefoot, charity shoes

saved for school. Come ginning season, bales
of cotton floated away, caressing
someone else's wife in a Sunday print,
blanketing babies too tender
for a father's calloused hand. Grandfather,

whatever words you had for me flicker
fading on the screen of memory, but still I hear you
on those nights when the black humus is grit
under my tongue, clotting my throat. As I claw

for words to fill the gaping ache, I picture you
pulling your children up from the dirt. Each night
you swallowed sorrow dark as sorghum
and rose the next day, ready to drop manna
into another waiting, moist mouth.

Hummingbird

for Freelin

She once loved watching the ruby-throated glow
through glass, though someone else fills feeders
now, and she can no longer see whirring
wings, the jeweled miracles humming along
an invisible string. You and your sisters flutter
about, whispering. A mother grown old,
living alone: it's a problem.

Sight gone, memory fading, she still regales
us with tales of mixing martinis and gossip
at parties, or family camping in the '62 wagon
with its tailgate tent. The past glows: nine decades
of nested gold. It's today's timetable she's lost
her grasp on, memory's wings flapping faster
and faster to land amid tangled branches.

And in these late days, she hums. No tuneful
bird song, but an automated drone, subconscious
om driving all she does. You try teasing her
out of it, and she laughs but can't seem to stop.
The hum goes on, like a bat's echolocation guiding
her twilight flight—or the heart's audible protest—
each breath an exhaled fury counting down time.

Zinnia Women

In 1910 sepia tones
he strokes smooth
the barrel of a borrowed gun,
leaning towards danger
in chaps and silk shirt.
Staring out at me, eyes
dark enough to fall for,
my grandfather poses.

But the Grandpa Horton I knew
in childhood sat flat-eyed
in a faded work shirt,
tobacco juice permanent
on his chin, reading Zane Grey.
Sometimes my grandmother
rocked next to him,
but most days she slipped
into her garden, tending
rows of phlox, larkspurs,
zinnias, a trumpet vine.

Sunday afternoons stretched out
like slow-shuffled dominoes,
Grandpa's game. We crowded
around a card table in the front room
crammed with two battered rockers,
Grandpa's cast-iron bed wedged
in the corner.

The one bedroom was sachet-
scented, garden-wafting,
Grandma's. I never wondered

over separate sleeping—
they were grandparents,
past all passion.

But then one day Grandma saw
a woman in her garden,
red-nailed, high-heeled,
preening among the zinnias.
Sunday visits got interesting
as women popped in and out
and Grandma tongue-lashed
Grandpa for bringing home those whores.

She called me to the window once
to witness, pointing out his sin.
But I saw red snapdragons and stood
bewildered, until Mama explained
that once the women had existed
outside my grandma's mind.

Mama told how my grandfather
disappeared for days
with his paycheck, spending it
on cheap whiskey and thin women,
and how, once, he plopped down
the price of a week's bread
and beans to dress up like a cowboy
and pose for that fancy photograph.

Several Sundays after that story,
we showed up as usual,
but I saw the corner bed
was gone. I turned, expecting
Grandpa to be absent, kicked out
at last. But there he sat

stroking dominoes, that black
photographic glitter back
in his eyes. No one mentioned
missing furniture, but Grandma
never saw another woman
outside her window.

And when she died
in the season of zinnias,
my grandfather cradled her,
delicate as dust-dry petals,
as they shared the same bed.

Fireflies

The past feels thicker here on the canyon floor,
ancient air filtering down. History hangs
over our heads as ancestral sin slows our steps.

In 1874, Rangers routed
Comanches at the Battle of Palo Duro:
repeating rifles dropped appaloosas and paints—
fourteen hundred—one by one. Each whinnying scream

echoed through this canyon as sun-stenched flesh
stacked ladders to heaven, the bleached bones
later a landmark guiding whites through grassland.

Those bones are long gone, but as darkness falls,
the fireflies come out, their cold glow the same light
that flickered witness above Comanche campsites.

I step soft among fireflies, the ground beneath me
a palimpsest of conquest: buffalo blood
and steaming scalps, gutted treaties, barbed wire,
paved roads to annihilation. The past pulses

underfoot, but the fireflies leave no mark.
Like flint sparking flame, they glimmer for the living
and the dead, glowing ghosts of moon-white bones.

Boys Would Come on Horses

for Jannica

This is what I remember
most about the night
she was born: the surprise
of her heat.

Lying coiled naked
on my slack belly,
her live weight
sizzled into mine,
and fourteen years now
she's burned right through me.

Once lately, we sat in the car
as she agonized
over making an entrance,
sure she was dressed wrong,
afraid of being laughed at.
I drove away leaving her
in pain so raw it was mine
all over again.

But these scars
are all incidental
blisters, gotten
only from being
so close to her own
tender searing,

until this evening.
I pull back the curtain,
see a palomino and a bay
casually owning my lawn.

Two riders take in the house.
One catches my eye
through the glass
and heat flares
along my borders.

He looks at me
with a boy face
but there's this man
hungriness about his limbs,
sliding down sweaty
flanks. I wonder
why boys and horses
I've never seen
are at my door.

But it's her they've come for.

She saunters
out to talk, born
knowing this would happen.
When did she learn slinging
back her head that way,
hair firing wild
all around, so much
blonde shrapnel?
Body turned
weapon,
she looks like

oh God.
She looks like
boys would come on horses.

After they've gone,
there's a quick call
to her best friend,
and she suddenly

(doesn't ask)
announces
they're going to the show.

To meet those boys?
She swears
that isn't so, is hurt
when I keep asking,
and the past burns
only a simmering echo
in this first flash fire.

I let her go
and worry the whole time
over the feel of him
even through glass and air.

Much later, kneeling
by her bed, I touch her
skin still
hot as the night
she was born.
She whispers,
so low it may be
imagined,
the boys weren't there.

Her hair's still splayed
reckless against
the pillow, but in glazed
dream light, it seems
more a Pre-Raphaelite halo,
making belief possible
for seconds at a time.

And I believe,
not in words,
but in a look that passes

between us, scattering
the shot
around our hearts
into ceasefire.
At least for tonight.

She understands now
what I don't trust—the heat
and something else she saw
in my eyes.

I breathe goodnight
into the spent ammunition
of her hair
and leave,
both of us knowing
I would have done anything
at fourteen
for boys who came on horses.

TWO

Real Estate Values

The blue, bent bicycle on the roof next door
stayed for a week
before someone yanked it down.
No neighborhood eyebrows raised,

just one more sign of property decline.
Their yard flutters with fast-food sacks
and dead toys; last week a tired ceramic cat
curled up cozy in ever-taller weeds.

Nothing too sacred for lawn ornament,
the five-year-old, locked out
for hours, clomps down the sidewalk
in dingy Scooby Doo briefs, scuffed cowboy boots

on the wrong feet. He makes a game
of darting behind my car every time
I back out. The girls, too young for Maybelline,
wear it anyway, swagger and brag

of tabloid boys slept with back in L. A.,
where they were rich, lived among the stars. Here,
the central air is broken and their windows,
open in the August swelter,

broadcast every slap. The kids
knock constantly, begging matches, a dollar,
a roll of scotch tape. My children call me cruel
when I lie, say we're all out.

They don't know how hard,
when that kid dares me in the driveway,
I have to bite my lip not to gun the motor,
run him down. How to explain it's more than the doorbell

at two a. m.? All along the property line, I dream
of drenching the air with fire,
as if rusted hubcaps and bruises
could be warded off by quarantine.

Flying Off the Overpass

Dreaming the incline too steep
I slam down hard
on gas, but the car
lets go
and I fall back through black air
forever before waking.

In daylight, that bridge sits
just outside Post, Texas, along
a ninety-mile stretch of Highway 84,
halfway
between a place where I am
scholar, writer, called by name,

and home,
hearing *Mom*
always once too often.
I yell at the kids to shut up,
go to sleep (please),
so I can study, then miss them
in a quiet house.

And sitting in class, I worry
the oldest forgot
lunch money, or that
my blue-eyed boy won't forget
I missed his school play.

Years from now,
when knife-bladed dark dreams
slide under their skulls,
will my children only know
I was always driving away?

And what if, one night,
my wheels touch the bridge
at the exact moment
the moon becomes full
and ripe enough to burst,
and I spin out to meet
dark

with one gleaming fang
and patches of fur
blossoming
down my back,
neither half of me knowing
on which side of the bridge
to fall.

Running Red Lights

Mama, you don't get the pull
of the center stripe
the way I do.

Standing by the freeway,
you don't understand the words
and there is no translation
for air sung from turning chrome,
for the humming union
of movement.

All my life, you've pulled
me back
from oncoming cars
worrying
one will run
me down.
And then, you ask,
What will become
of your babies?

I don't know, Mama.

My lungs are ash
with taking in used air
and living under wrong
names.

On this road
there is no
good mother,
sweet wife.

But there is breathing.

Tonight, I dance
in traffic.
Stepping out slow
and shoeless,
I waltz among
rushing silver fenders,
flirt with glinting
headlights.

Danger
slides away, spinning
in gravel.

Mama, don't you know?

My feet feel right
on this highway
and I can outrun
any red car.

Break Time at El Rancho

Sit down, honey. Here—take a drag
off my cigarette. First day's hard, I know.
You want some advice? Keep the coffee comin',
counters clean, and don't waste time
on the women. They ain't gonna tip much
anyway—you're too damn cute. Nah, you gotta

concentrate on men. Swing your ass,
just a little, every time you go by,
watch them tips pile up. You get it swaying
and stay here long, you might find somebody
who'll want you to shine him the way you polish
that table, if you know what I mean. Yeah.

That's how I met husband number two,
cocktailing over in Big Spring at The Stampede.
God, his Levi's were so tight you couldn't slip
a hand in his back pocket if you tried.

We'd get them four swamp coolers going
full blast in the middle of July—
there wasn't no place more fun—cowboys
pouring in by the pickup load. You look
at those shitkickers just right, their hands
rummaging around in some girl's lap,

you'd still get a pretty big tip. 'Specially
if you didn't mind a little pinch on the butt
now and then. Bob played in a band
with Hoyle Nix and the boys.
I still remember him—fingering
that bass guitar—winking at me every time

I went by. Got so I'd go outta my way,
walk by the bandstand just for that wink.
Pretty soon he's scribblin' notes on napkins,
commentin' on his dreams, and I'm a goner.

Nothing to do but climb in his truck
and drive straight through the night to Juarez
singing *Vaya con Dios* all the way.
I come back with a young'n in the chute,
but Bob, he up and left when the band did,
didn't even stay around to see if it was a boy.

Here's a picture of my kid. I tell him
he looks like his daddy. Makes him feel
better: he thinks Bob died in a ten-car
pile-up. That sonofabitch—likely still
sprouting seed from Dallas to Tucumcari.
He never even bought me a ring.

I got the kid; he got a tattoo—*Louise*—
plain as day, right across the top
of his butt. I like to think of that
when I ain't made five dollars all night

and my feet cramp up, just muse
on some old girl coming across my name
in the throes of passion. Makes up for a world
of pinchin'.

Tips

The boy's mother visited,
like a favorite aunt, brought him all
her tips in a fat Mason jar
so full of dimes and quarters
that when she dumped it in his lap,
the weight lay heavy and hard,

almost like love. He rubbed the face
from a lucky dime under the covers,
spent hours stacking, sorting,
counting each coin
an omen of her return.

What makes a mother leave
a nine-year-old in the back booth
of El Rancho Café, waiting
in corduroy, wondering
for years if it was him
or just the drumming black hole

in her head? Everything was his
after she collapsed at Red's Grill,
third week into a new job. He kept her purse
the longest, spilling its clues
like money—rhinestoned glasses,
some "Larry's" number, scuffed Bufferin

for two-day migraines. The boy
dreamed her born stepping into pink
cotton poplin in the closet,
Louise already stitched tight
across her breast. And when the blood
burst bright in her head,

he wondered if a mother could know
all she left as the glass jar
shattered. He longed for a final kiss,
clutched pennies minted
before he was born.

A History for Louise

for Louise Northerns and her son J. T. Northerns, 1948-1993

The space between letters on any headstone,
yours or his, for instance, is limited. Sharp
carving delineates the number of days
with a hyphen between *born* and *died*, the messy
living in between blown away by a stonecutter's

breath. There's only so much room to read
between the lines, but the palimpsest of spaces
holds the history of your son. He kept your purse
and cheap rings, a few wrinkled dresses, the divorce
decrees, in a battered box—chased after you

by flunking out of college and quitting any job
he was good at. Always, he wondered how I could love him,
a boy you didn't bother to name. He worried in the dark,
that like you, he would die young, that all your flaws
were his. And when he gave me your gaudy topaz

ring, I hid it in the velvet lining
of my jewelry box, not caring what a mother-in-law,
dead before I met her son, might have for me. Only now
do I see how alike we really are. You've left me
the spaces. Understand, Louise,

that a space is as hollow as your coffin
after all these years, an empty place opening up
around bones that have shifted and settled,
leaving room for snatches of "Be my Baby"
on the radio to shatter me with his tenor

singing along, room for the fragrance of frying chicken
to trigger an image of him watching me
bread wings and thighs the night
I announced my leaving. I picture you
carefully straightening a little boy's plaid jacket

before you left him in a back booth and I know
he floated back ever after when you least expected it—
his nine-year-old grin interrupting a night out
with the girls, his granite headstone
slipping up beside your own.

Plate Tectonics

Wedding shower sheets and china
filled our new house.
We stumbled through
an abundance of love
wildly the first years,
believing
no matter how many plates broke,
there would always be
service for two.
Good linen smoothed
out the terrain
of a second-hand bed,
and wrapped in crisp cotton,
we wallowed.

But later, making our bed
I searched for sheets not stained
or worn and found
the drawer empty.
After fifteen years
of dinner from unmatched plates
and tarnished silver, we slipped
silent through the house,
stepping over growing faults
in the floor.

The rose-shaded lamp
that came wrapped
in wedding dove paper
with a card for luck
and ultimate love
had a short in it now,
so we talked in the dark,

he and I, late one night,
too late. Voice so used
it came out a sigh,
I said, *Things wear out*,
and slowly heaved
myself up to go.

All original words lost
along with silver's shine,
he called after me,
Don't let the door
hit you on the way out.
It didn't. Unoiled
hinges rasped and caught—
no resounding crash
or closing slam.
Denied a decent exit, I sank
back into bed. And miles apart
on this continent of fraying sheets

we drifted

to sleep.

Floaters

for Dr. Jim Jury

You've got floaters! the eye doc proclaims,
as if you've just won the Mega Millions
Power Ball. It's nothing to worry about,
just another little nasty surprise of aging,
like that first gray pube, or mottled splotches
blooming overnight on the back of the hand.

Floaters? Isn't that also the name for dead bodies,
submerged and bloating, slowly rising into sight?

These floaters are a different kind of dead:
the vitreous humor of the eye shrinking,
shredding, cobwebby strands dancing at the edge
of vision, microscopic astronauts out
for a dreamy spacewalk around eye's orbit.
You're in luck, the doctor says, delivering
what passes for good news at this age:

it could be worse. No bright flashes to signal
a detached retina, blindness, sudden dark.

Still, the inky smudges dart and bounce,
impossible to stare down but always there,
lurking reminders of how hard
the body works to reach escape velocity.
Pieces pull free, slough off; veins bulge and sag;
bladder muscles give way, so that stray sneezes
send a dribble down the leg, each new discovery
dumping sludge into this river of loss.

No, it's nothing to worry about, simply
a preview of a time to come when the vessel
that is you, a ship decommissioned
and condemned for salvage in dry dock,
is stripped clean to bones and teeth

and you are detached and floating in the corner
of what you once thought was God's eye.

Keeping Watch as My Ex-Husband Dies

I stare out the window, remembering
walks to the last soda fountain on the square
for breakfast those Saturday mornings,
our hands twined so tight it was hard to hold
the paper sack. From his hospital bed,
my ex-husband calls *What are you looking at?*,
wants to know what he's missing.

Just thinking of those fountain Cokes and doughnuts
from Stinson's Drug, I say. *Remember walking*
down the street, sugar on our mouths? He frowns.

He is young enough to recall the taste
of first dates, but doesn't. Doesn't even remember
our kids' names when I tell him how our boy
sat the bench at yesterday's Little League game.

What he remembers instead is last night's dream
of a Nazi death camp, how I left him there.
And now as night falls, he begs me not to go.
How to tell him? He was in a war,
but not that one. No context for his memory
but the heartbreak of my actual leaving years ago.

Those early mornings we drank our Cokes
from to-go cups, too young for coffee, ice chilling
doughnut glaze to grease slick in the back of my throat.

Now a sticky film coats his brain
as he searches for words, waste water
swirling up in black-bubbled aphasia
so that he spits out *Please, I need a drink*
of thirsty. I hand him the glass, and as it shatters
to the floor, I stare once more out the window

but find against sunset's glare dust motes streaming
into a reflecting pool of transgression: years I spent
back-pedaling, pulling away, leaving him in the dust,
dust that now waits to reclaim, settle him down
into the long dark furrow to come. He doesn't ask again
and I don't say that I am making a list of all he will miss.

Last Breath

for JTN, 1948-1993

Left alone in this room
for a private goodbye,
I held you for the last time
in starch and harsh light.
Your fingertips already cooling,
I stretched across your still
heart, our clustered chests
warm, and held on.

My hospital stays birthed
our children, who slid
into your arms slick,
pink-sueded. Today, I pushed
your mouth shut, and air
wheezed out, almost human.

I did not hope breath back
or wish you one minute more
of the slow morphine drip,
though all you've left me
is knowing that you're gone,
my mouth a hollow O.

Mother-Daughter Dresses

I refused to buy them when she was a toddler—
the lace-trimmed polished cottons and matching
taffetas. But now we slip in and out
of one another's closets, taking all

we can. She finds me listening to her music
but forgives me, for it's Nirvana, and this night
Kurt Cobain is dead. She settles beside me
and we whisper a eulogy to "Heart-shaped Box"
and "Come as You Are." I describe how her dad and I

did this, turned the lights down, played music
making words more than flesh, the night we heard
John Lennon died. We sing around the real worry—
the iconography shading her remaining days—

her father, last spring, at church front
in his shimmering blue coffin, heavy
American flag from a Viet Nam tour draped
across his best brown tweed. The flag, folded
into a perfect trinity, filled her hands,

but still she clutched the rough lapels
of her daddy's jacket. Tonight, she says I'm sloshing
gin and tonic on the carpet, so I go to bed,
leaving her to the silent six hundred seconds

ending Cobain's "Nevermind," straining for secret tracks.
I'm afraid she knows she won't find them. Friends bear
mascara smudges like ashes, as if they've lost a lover or a god,
but for her it's only another prop pulled, just as mine fall away
when I open the liquor cabinet to find

she's watered the vodka one more time. At sixteen,
this daughter looks nothing like me, yet every day
she edges closer to the fit. Dresses
slip over our shoulders, come floating down.

THREE

Driving Back from Bandolier

Time for lunch, my tongue already tasting
New Mexico green, we slow in Los Alamos.
As we drive through town, I blink in surprise
at street signs: *Trinity, Oppenheimer, Bikini Atoll.*

In search of parking, we come upon crowds,
picnic baskets, blankets spread on the grass.
Buckets and buckets of sunflowers surround a pond,
blossoms exploding on my retina in a golden flare.

What day is this? We ask, suddenly grasp
Hiroshima's pall. Taste of chile verde fades
as a scorched memento mori settles
on my tongue, yellow burst blotting out the sun.

Breaking City Ordinances

Black Cats and bottle rockets
are illegal in Albuquerque.
But here on the eve,
young boys toss and run
and firecrackers pop
past midnight, reminding me
of all things forbidden:
this weekend,
this man in my arms.

Fourth of July morning, we drive
miles to the reservation, climb
red rock so high we are breathless
in newer altitudes. But no height
lets me forget the ex-husband I left
behind in a hospital room, pieces
sliced away in biopsy, his body
closing down.

Traveling back to Albuquerque
after dark, my new lover and I
catch the tail-end of silent
fireworks in every little town
we pass, quiet explosions
that trail us all the way.

I think again
of the other man.
Though we have been apart
for years, his invading cells
track me down, greedy
tracer rockets homing in.

In my harder moments, I think
he has chosen this: played
his last card by folding.
And I should give up, too.

But then we are past all fireworks
and city lights explode
before me. In that glittering
power surge, I know
I cannot be cast back to earth
with a path so skyward.

Powder tamped, fuse ignited,
blue constellations brew
within me. Soon, globed
lightning will shoot
from my eyes, and I will rise,
spitting stars.

I wave my hand across the sky
and fingers trail luminescent
strands, the way sparklers sear
the retina of childhood
Fourth of July,
the way this lover's tongue
paints my body tonight.

Snake Trails

Watching your prairie rattler,
there is this luxury in sharing
a room with danger, the power
of opening the black hinged lid
of his cage, of touching
diamond-slick smoothness,
hard-muscled enthrallment,
black tongue fluid
and fast. But still,
he's on the other side
of the glass.

And you, his owner, reptilian
cool, you side-wind hard
through cold-chiseled days,
until warmed a little while
by a human body, mine.
After love, you pull back
into a morning of paper
and coffee.

The day separates
into glass
and walls, houses
and streets,
until a whole town
snakes between us.
Each time I fight
my way back.

Slip out
my front door, curve
around, whip down 37th,
that long fast

stretch, my heart coiled,
never sure—
will you let me in?
The traffic light,
two more blocks, a left,
slide down your street,
holding my breath, always
expecting another woman's
car in your drive,
her bumper snugged up
next to yours.

Even in your house,
pretending I am safe
under the sheets,
you inside me,
I never forget
hardly anyone
keeps danger
so close so long
without giving in.

I wake in darkened
hunger, touch my tongue
to yours, just once,
feel the flicker.
Wrap shed skin
around me, your other self
cast off casual,
as if anyone
could do it. Feel
your cool smoothness
pull me in, drying taut,
tightening,
and I am on your side
of the glass.

Shedding

Mostly the animals dream
of other animals.
There are exceptions . . .
                    —from "Dreams of the Animals," Margaret Atwood

After years weighted down with rocks
and poems, he's talking,
tongue darting, saying more
than you will. I read Atwood aloud to him:

> *the silver fox in the roadside zoo*
> *dreams of digging out*

and wonder if your tawny prairie rattler
knows dreaming. Caged years ago
in New Mexico by you and another
woman, what can he know but glass

observation? You left that woman in a canyon,
brought the snake, taped shut,
to Texas. And when you finally took me,
last summer, to the Guadalupe Box, one touch

of granite, same shade as your snake,
let me know every fall's talk
of letting him go is only a dream, assuming
snake homesickness. His cage holds all

you've boxed up for me, domestic
at last. You lose people so easily,
why can't you shed
the snake? Do you think he asks

so much less? He's asking so much
of me right now
(slick, fine,
hypnotizing),

I want to lift him out
barehanded. I fingerprint
the glass against his flicker,
read to him of how

the iguana
in the petshop window . . . ruling
its kingdom of water-dish and sawdust
dreams of sawdust.

Quivering among corn husks, he's newly shed
tonight. Year after year, he slips skin
blending into rock and your memory of river
in a country before me. Let his last days

imagine us
sliding loose down shale
in search of the one hot,
perfect dream.

Tornado Vision

You never bothered to steer
your way through love
or the weather, just twisted
down to Texas, storm speed
clearing a path. On first sight, I loved
how I had no choice, how your whirling
force pulled me into the tangle
of the funnel cloud.

Even now, you persist in seeing every sky
gone green, your rusted tongue hinged
on danger's copper twang
as you wait for twisters to rip
you off course, set you down
on new ground, everything open
again. You think sweeping up pieces
is all that's left
for us: damage control.
Remember planning escape

when the big one hit?
You said we'd slide
under Deep Creek bridge, simmer
in the mud, the rest of the town
blowing down. Meet me halfway now
under that bridge, as sirens roar.
In this whirling wreckage
we are the eye,
and we'll cut a fine wide door
through the storm.

Halloween, Albuquerque

Armed with dull knives and Budweiser,
we convene on Pat's front porch for this ritual
of carving flesh. We each choose a face,
a personal totem against encroaching
ghosts. I plunge
into pumpkin, scoop seeds, carve stars
for eyes. Pat swirls inventive curls,
and Tom, out of practice fifty years,
settles for triangles. Only Bill

hovers over his work, hesitating,
willing each slice of the knife
just right. Like all else he does,
it's got to be the jack-o'-lantern
of the century. He cuts,
frowns, flings pumpkin all around,
finally quits, saying it looks
too much like him. He's left
just enough skin for hooded eyes,
snarling teeth. The whole face

peels back to raw moist pulp,
so thin this pumpkin's candle-soul
will glow over the whole night.
The party starts and arriving guests
agree, pronounce his pumpkin best,
scariest. He's still not convinced
as we go inside for Jack Daniels
and horror stories, and somewhere in between
my third drink and Pat's tale
of Navaho ghost dogs, I notice Bill's gone.

Through the window, I see him crouched,
candle blown out. No jack-o'-lantern
can stop the demons who hold court
in his head, come three a. m. Night
after night he carves the dark. He gouges,
slashes, always trying for the ultimate cut,
the wicked smile that will fool us all
into mistaking him
for God. We half-believe
already, but that is never enough.

Coming Out of Rough Creek Canyon

I dream of Mexico beaches or nights
along the river walk—a destination.
As usual, you won't commit to anything
until it happens. There's no talk
of tomorrow or where we'll be
a year from now.

I press for a plan; you say
you'll surprise me,
but last summer, camping on the Llano,
you brought no food, not even a pan
for the fish we caught. I fumed,

but if we had stopped to cook,
we'd have missed that armadillo
just off the path, moonlight
glinting on tarnished armor,
a found coin in the dark.

So, this time, I wait and see.
Sunday, you pull me into the jeep
and we head northeast down back roads,
find Cottonwood Flat
and Little Rough Creek.
We wind through red clay canyons
caught in clear March light,
the air tinged with old music.

Settling into the day, I inhale
fields fresh with winter rye,
just ripened to the shade
of sex. We drive every road,
and you, the newcomer to this land,

take me places
I've never been, though we don't
even cross the county line.

This morning, that same strong light
slants through bedroom blinds
and sprawls across our hearts.
I know there's no plan
for this day or next year.

But I recall yesterday—the way
we suddenly twisted out of the canyon
and up on to the flatland.
You turned to me and smiled,
and there before us
lay a red dusted carpet of a road,
unfurled all the way to forever.

Anniversary

for Bill

Like a sestina, marriage is a closed form
of rules and order, places and time bound
by vows spoken in hope of sidestepping wounds
of ugly grammar, the common cliché. But a door
closed by a wedding somehow allows entry to the heart's
core for the careless, or perhaps careful, word that sparks,

not edifying fire, but scarring rage. Embers spark
arguments a decade old and form
turns formulaic, shaping the heart
into a red-edged cliché as we are bound
in a repeating pattern behind that closed door.
We learned the pattern long ago as it wound

its way along a map of hurt. Now we rip old wounds
again, just because we can, knowing that a spark
can kindle a flame, or a flame-thrower. That door
closes out strangers and the strange, but true to form,
holds in every word as all hurt is bound
in our book of memory, embedded in heart

pulse, accumulating weight and heft. Heart-
sick, we bury the pile of daily wounds
in a stack with too many bills, unpaid, bound
to spill out when the account is low and spark
snide remarks, words we'd reform
or rephrase for anyone outside that door.

This years-long poem is just you and me, and the door,
we know, opens in or out. So the heart
handles the added weight of jibes and sneers, forms
imperfect, daily and clichéd. Wound
together, we are so twined that even warring sparks
tighten the shared history of a sestina bound

by a thousand daily lines. But the bounds
also hold secret signs, allowing the door
of desire to open the moment you lean over me, sparked
simply by gray curls haloing about your head. My heart
backtracks to that night I first wound
up in your arms. Running down the street, a form

of recklessness sparked by the dark cord that bound
my heart tighter than rhyme, I wound up at your door.
We began with words, and my world found form.

A Texas Girl on Central Avenue

The plane touches down in Albuquerque
and we drive through the old part
of town where adobe is trimmed in pure
turquoise sky or rose-dusted
mesa, where great lobes of dark chiles
shine welcome.

Next morning, fresh
from Bible-Belt West Texas,
I walk down Central Avenue,
old Route 66, gawking at girls
with nose rings, loving it
when dark tattooed men whistle
and call after me, *Hey, Babe!*
Meandering through tourist shops
in search of Indian trinkets,
I hear a harmonica, some rich liquid
blues tune running quicksilver
down the street.

Around the corner, a street musician
and his girl sit against a wall,
wanting nothing more
than to play for me all day.
Too cheap to throw coins
their way, I window-shop,
walking back and forth
just to hear that sound.
Finally, I duck into a store,
choose earrings from Taiwan
for my little girl, deeming local
silver too expensive.

Back in Texas, my daughter loves
the gaudy shine of dime-store trash,
never missing what I couldn't buy:
that harmonica's hard throb sliding
through me before it hit the street.

Sparks

It used to be me charging hard down dark
streets to a lover's arms. And it was me
talking poetry and politics
in his office as we shut out sirens,
first faint, then loud. Emerging hours after
the noise died down, we found one corner
of campus smoldering and soaked,
fire spent, trucks and the arsonist long gone.

But tonight, it's you, daughter, eyeing your beloved
in secret code. Telegraphed sparks aren't mine
to know or hold, but I recall this giddy
room-tilting spin you're in, the two of you
clothed in a force field conjured by heart's
magnetic north, while outside, whole kingdoms
are born, rise up, and burn to the ground.

Flying Fish

for Jordan

Only this boy, just turned ten,
can disrupt our Sunday
paper squabbles
as he rushes from lake
to back door, showing off
his catch. We look up,
expecting a perch at line's
end. Instead: a sudden rhythmic

WHUP, WHUP, WHUP,

and a catfish whirls around
the ceiling fan. My son drops down
on one knee, yelling I'm sorry!
 I'm sorry! as he ducks each spin
of the fish, knowing
he's done it again.

Only this boy finds trouble
so often—just last week
the note sent home—failing fifth-
grade science. But he knows
sky's Orion and the depth
of the Mariana Trench,
knows mating habits of ten
kinds of fish, including this one,
circling, amazed, above us all.

Only this boy, the teacher says,
forgets answers straight
from the book. It's a failure
to pay attention, follow

directions. I look at this boy now,
dodging a catch he's somehow hooked
to the sky. There are fifth-grade
teachers trolling obvious waters,
and there is my son,
casting his line into the clean
unknown, never worrying

the hook may fall back
on him. Who will save the world
from filled-in blanks? Only this boy.

Hammock Psalm

Precariously strung, you and I forge a bed
in a canted hammock, after years
of improbable physics. We want dark,
our bodies singing psalms to calm cradle
play—the way you tip your beer, trickle fizz
down my shirt—but street light's hypnotic hold

is our only star, too bright to hold
backyard secrets. You shotgun the light from bed
in dreams, sprinkle crackled glass fizz
before me, but the raw glare of this year's
new union crunches underfoot—you've wed cradle
as well as hand—you have married the dark.

My children climb through windows of this dark,
the girl's crumpled screen an escape from our hold.
You're not the father sanding their cradle
boards in the photograph album. That bed
and its maker belong to other years
visible only in the floating fizz

of memory. They wake to a widening fissure
that chases their father's face into the dark
each time you make them smile. As though the years
you've spent with us were sabotage, they hold
you hostage, finger the safety catch from bed
to window, aim stinging shots that cradle

and slice through cords, unraveling this cradle,
hammock strung too wide between trees. The leaves' fizz
whispers that we're never alone in bed,
and you long to tangle limbs in the dark
with me, just once, without having to hold
your breath, but here's the boy, eleven years

old, asking, *You guys staying out here for years?*
I bite my tongue as you pull back, cradle
your beer, tight-roped. You lean to him and hold
open your side of the hammock. Ropes fizz
and twist with all our weight, but you tell the dark
ghost stories he loves, and he sails in to bed.

And then, you close my eyes to years of streetlight fizz
and tell me as we cradle in tangled dark
that what we hold will fill this hollow bed.

FOUR

My Brothers Teach Me What It Means to Grow Up Male in West Texas

Fondling stashed firecrackers, boys root around
in the dirt for any live thing to ride
in the green plastic Army Jeep: roly
poly bugs, woolly worms, generic black

beetles. All get *vroomed* down the path with thrills
of testosterone, and I cover ears
against the blast, a roadside IED
of Black Cats, passengers surprised by flash

and bang. A satisfying crunch of beetle's
cracked carapace, but brothers like woolly
worms best for this game, their yellow and green
guts splattering such satisfying stains.

These caterpillars will never wear black
and white dotted wings of great leopard moths,
won't open like feathery kites to dry
under a Texas sun. But I don't grieve

what they won't become. No, I miss the way,
just hours before, we'd let them tickle
up and back the length of our arms, gentle
friends I've now betrayed, not quite knowing how.

She is a Secret

She is a secret waiting to be spilled
    over afternoon mojitos muddled
with mint. She is the mint leaf's fancy dress

    of a caterpillar's cocoon, and
she is the cocoon of childhood's frayed
    blanket. She is a blanket stuffed

in the broken window in the last
    room of the last motel on the interstate.
She is the motel you had to double back

    and find in the rain, and she is the rain
that chills you to the bone in twilight's
    shade. She is the shade casting shadow

puppets through a chain link fence, and she
    is the chain anchoring a ship
that has long since sailed. She is the sail

    catching wind of a fevered dream,
and she is your dream vacation
    on a poster behind glass. She is the glass

box you break in case of emergency,
    and she is the emergency exit
you don't take, knowing you'll tumble

    down stairs into the leaf-green day
before yesterday, where she waits,
    a secret you will never spill.

About Those Shoes . . .
(Cinderella's Manifesto)

I love my Jimmy Choos, but where and when,
I choose, not you. I've shed shoes, not to leave
behind a trail of blistered crumbs or blood-
tinged prints for you to find, vestige of heart

lopped to fit, no, not to tease or lead you on,
but to sprint through a dark forest of possible
ruin, starring at last in my own neon-lit
action flick. Unhobbled, unspiked, unstilted,

my toes grip ground, soak up dirt's current,
ancient tales feeding my feet as bright ancestral
arrows pulse out a path. I pause, let tendrils
caress instep, curl around calf. A vine

shoots up my spine, trellis to the sky.
Climbing that ladder through the window
of sunrise, I kiss my own waking. Only then
do I let my hair down and slip into those shoes.

Hiding in the Forest of July

for Cassandra Jane at three

Animal armies arrayed across the rug,
she slides a plastic puma safely
from sight of prying tigers.
I am hiding in the Forest of July,
her proxy growls.

Her heart's sweet bee buzz
powers dragonfly eyes
as she marches gazelles
across a glade shaded
by the oak coffee table.

At the park, swing's singing chains
hurl her skyward. Legs powering
a rocket ship
through the Milky Way,
she aims for stars light years away
from the forest's slow fade
to a bareboned tree.

Joseph Mans the Swings

He pulls weighted chains, cinches each child tight,
smoothing the belt too long
on a chubby three-year-old. It's not

what you think. He shelves them with a wink
and starts the machine ratcheting,
spinning them for a minute and fifteen seconds

of potent machine-oil air, sticky-sweet
lyrics swaying them 'round and 'round
and always back to him. On slow nights

or just when he really needs it, he palms
the metal lever until it scalds
his hand, whirling the blue-eyed baby

that will never be his longer and longer
until she's almost sick with thrill and he knows
he is the only one. Parents in the crowd

wonder, in just that second before he slows
the arc, if they will get their children back. The scratchy
soundtrack muddies the music as their babies

fly by, the ground spinning like a wrecked
dance floor beneath them. For Joseph, they blur
into a pool of light, tunnel of love,
with his hand only at the master switch.

My First Year Teaching Seventh-Grade English

We'd just invaded Iraq, and giddy
jingoism flooded limbic systems,
though it thinned and faded by the back row
where Ernesto's head lolled in weedy haze.
The principal came for him on the day
we were outside writing down all we saw

and heard. *We all see the world differently,*
I explained, as Ernesto was herded
inside like a cow doomed to the kill chute
at Sunflower Beef, where his parents worked nights.
Back in class, I tried salvaging the time;
talked power and language, swaying phrases.

Poking at their boredom, I risked going
too far, asked: *The war, for instance, is it
really connected to 9/11?*
My strategy worked too well and Stevie
shouted, *Let's nuke 'em!* Rowdy choruses
of *Yeah! Yeah! Let's nuke em!* jostled the calm.

Taylor B. jumped up on his desk. *My dad
has an AK-47!* he yelled.
All had opinions as talk of revenge
awakened ancient reptilian brains,
all but Ernesto, who was down the hall,
cuffs snapped shut around his snake-thin brown wrists.

When I think back on that day, I marvel
at the sudden eruption of primal
bloodlust. Did any boy, so quick to pick
foreign fights, sign up for a war or two?
And what about Ernesto? Did he grow
into those handcuffs, claim them as his own?

I lost track of that class long ago, all
but Taylor B. I see him at Kwik Stop
or the hardware store now and then. See his
trigger finger twitching in his pocket,
muscle memory of a severed tail. His
white-boy swagger, concealed-carry smile,
the sure truth of no one coming for him.

Pronoun Reference

A teacher and a nonbinary student
walk into a bar . . .
wait, no—scratch that.

A nonbinary student walks into my Comp I
classroom and tells that joke, but it falls flat
on classmates new to gender-fluid terms.
Still, they quickly accept this wise-cracking
self-proclaimed *they* as one of them,
all struggling to stay afloat amid oceans
of verb tense errors and comma splices.

Pronouns mean little to this group
except points on a grammar quiz, but I fret
for weeks over the looming review
of pronoun agreement: *Singular nouns*
take singular pronouns; plural takes plural . . .

Then we'll get to the part that throws them:
The way we talk is wrong, using the plural "they"
to refer to singular "everyone," for instance . . .

These mostly first-gen students, who find
the waters of English muddier than the Rio Grande,
will trust me as arbiter of the rules,
even as I explain how language changes
over time, rules lagging behind, ice-age old
conventions thawing slow as glaciers
edging towards doom.

They'll be confused by rules that are not rules,
so I ponder the time to spring this surprise,
secretly hoping my *they* will be absent,

solving my own pronoun dilemma.
But as I make copies of the handouts,
somewhere within me, the waters stir and shift.

I picture this singular student, wry and brassy
in their combat boots and tats, and the roil
within me stills and settles. I stop copying.
And just like that, the polar ice caps of language
melt away, flooding these dry Kansas plains
with a welcome sea change in praise of *they*.

Lines

A truck crosses the center line
in California, crashing into lives.
Twin sisters part ways; one lives,
one dies. Closer to home, a Kansan

faces news cameras, grieving slain son
and dad. Wrong place, wrong time—
lined up like shooting gallery ducks,
stunned prey for a crazed hater's gun.

News of the world
is sorrow of this world,
someone else's pain

until the phone buzzes
by your bed, snake's midnight
hiss slicing before and after,
a cold streak of indelible ink.

Wake Up Call

Three men face domestic terrorism charges for allegedly plotting to
bomb an apartment complex occupied by Somali immigrants in
southwest Kansas, the US Department of Justice said Friday.
                                        —CNN, Oct. 17, 2016

In the back room of Kansas they plot
holy war, target apartments one town over—
home to Somali *cockroaches*—
a make-shift mosque the final straw of insult.

Conspiracy theories drill their rumpled
brains like a right-wing lobotomy, ice pick
behind the eye chiseling rage:

We need to wake people up! Use a bow
on them cockroaches and dip it in pig's blood.
Ain't gonna be nothing nice about it.

At the community college across town, two sisters
in hijab master English grammar and write
of Somalia: milking goats after school, warm foam
swirling in cups of tea like clouds in a bright African sky.

They don't write of famine or war or tell
how one sister, child bride years ago, longs
for the children she left behind. When news breaks
of the foiled attack, the sisters remain unafraid.

These girls have seen worse than middle-aged
white guys playing out fumigation fantasies,
but the terrorists have done a number
on those of us with padlocked American lives.

We are wide awake now. A leaky faucet
we mistook for insomnia, their words drop
down—*plop—plop—plop*—each ripple
an echoing shiver in the far-edged river of dark:

kick in the doors
and kill them one by one
slowly with a silencer
even the one year olds

Opening Night

The roughneck, nineteen, on a drilling rig
two years already, scuffs mud from steel-toed
boots, ducks into the smoky blue buzz
of the 250 Club. Twirls his girl
to Merle Haggard classics, shoots a little pool,

only wants two-stepping to Saturday night's
routine. She whispers, *Carnival's in town,*
and he slaps back a *No,* but she wheedles,
*C'mon, win me one of them big pink
gorillas . . . like you done for Missy.*

The squirrel cages and the tilt-a-whirl unfold
like neon Georgia O'Keeffe dahlias on a paved
parking lot, as *Do the Locomotion* outblares
someone's bawling brat. In a faded trailer
a carney's tube top exposes rolls

of cotton candy flab as she points out
stuffed monkeys chomping felt bananas,
giant pandas and the coveted gorilla
vying for top-shelf billing. Nine soft-ball pitches later
he's managed only a papier-mâché rose

and a wrenched arm. She sulks onto the Zipper
behind him and clings to her side of the cage,
though every toss of the ride slides him
right to her. Centrifugal force
is no match for blossoming teenage scorn

and he stumbles aground, funnel cake
rumbling with Budweiser in his belly.
Heaving a stream onto July-hot asphalt,
he leaves first vomit of the night,
like fresh roadkill, steaming heat.

Thanksgiving in Liberal, Kansas

The slaughterhouse breeze matches the man
standing on the corner between Dillons
and the cash machine. In wrinkled jeans, he leans
on a walking stick, clutches a rough
cardboard sign, fingernails edged in grime. The sign's
error jumps out: *Any help will be thankful.*
I cringe, wanting to rip his cardboard
grammar in a red-pen rage.

I've read panhandlers touch rocky hearts
by freezing in November rain, whispering
without words: *throw money—I'll go away.*
He'll take any help? Would he thank me
for correcting his grammar in place of a pillow
or a trip to the ATM? Tonight he'll count
hundred-dollar handouts in a room glowing
with others' guilt. Maybe. Maybe he's a cheat,

a fox, a thief. Or maybe he's simply
what he seems: down on his luck, no chance
to land in another time or place,
ever. That radioactive image
of him juggles into my sleep, wakes me
at 3 a.m., dribbling guilt's fallout
into Thanksgiving's pumpkin pies
waiting to be baked.

Undone

This obsession with undoing
all, your finger running down
a page, ticking off a list,
has now landed here, in Kansas,
on my students: DACAs who want
only a driver's license and a dream.

They tread water, trying to touch ground
as they straddle a line their parents crossed
for them, parents who now work the kill floor
at Sunflower Beef, hacking hundred-pound slabs
of meat in a freezing fluorescent vault so
their children may grow on this side of the line.

These dreamers have names: Edgar, Teresa, Juan—
but to you, they are just a list of un:
undocumented, unwhite, un-us, (*illegal
rapists and thugs*). As you brandish threats
like a loaded hard-on or a gun, they wait
for a knock at the door, the sound
of all hope and change coming undone.

The Promised Land

Garish plastic Redskin shines by sunset
on the high school wall. 'Cross town, Sunflower Beef
smokestacks glow like the Star in the East,
lighting the way for Mexican pilgrims

up Highway 54 to Western Crest
Trailer Park. Night's temperature inversion
holds that glow, clamps down a red bowl over
the whole town. You smell it then, mist of blood

and burning bone rising from the kill floor.
Workers shiver in company-issue
coats, flaying sides of beef they can't afford.
For them, tripe and menudo and children,

their sons' and daughters' *futball* forbidden
at Redskin Field—American heaven
reserved for Friday nights, Jesus blessing
every kick, every tackle, every pass.

FIVE

Someone Found

Texan Cynthia Ann Parker was kidnapped by Comanches at age nine in 1836 and lived with them until 1860, when she was recaptured by Texas Rangers. During her twenty-four years with the Comanches she married war chief Peta Nocona and bore him three children. Peta Nocona gave her the Comanche name Nautdah, which means "Someone Found."

—from *Empire of the Summer Moon*
by S. C. Gwynne

Rangers yanked her, so covered in buffalo
blood and guts, only blue eyes gave her away.
They brought her back to picket fences and hot water,
a Bible and a corset to shore up her soul.

Nautdah wept for her boys, not yet warriors, lost
in the raid. Were they wandering vast grasslands
alone? Or, like their father, gone for good,
bones smoldering in ashes of rage?

White words stuck in her throat; starched calico weighed
her down like a shroud. She fled, Prairie Flower
on her hip, baby toes swaddled in mother-stitched
moccasins, beads glinting by North Star's light.

Caught, brought back, she ran again. And again.
Locked up each time by family astounded
at a captive who did not want saving,
Nautdah whispered Comanche prayers

into daughter's dark hair. She wept for wisdom
but did not wait for a sign as her fleeing feet
pounded this message into the ground:
you cannot rescue someone already found.

The Playwright's Daughter

for Mary Alice

On her second divorce from the same husband,
a man who loves her enough to want her
dead, she can still laugh. We burn
the phone wires with our talk of men.
I ask why her new man isn't working out;
she says, *Hon, if I can't picture his head
between my legs right off, then something's wrong.*
She can do that: sum up all my pale rhetoric

in one red line. It's how she's gotten by
since her famous father left her, three years old,
in the West Texas town he satirized all the way
to Broadway. One night, after we've been drinking
five hours straight, she pulls out the magazines,
reads me his reviews. She knows writing
is in her blood, but could she be that good?

And what about how her dad roman-candled
to the top, then wrote three flops, drank
himself dead at forty-one? *I guess I worry
too much,* she giggles. *First,
I have to get famous.* She writes a little
while she waits for the ex-husband
to come after her, or worse,
the kids. Shows her work around,

never sends it off. Her poems stack up
in the closet, or sit locked
in the computer she pawned for cigarette
money. She swings on the front porch
after midnight, foot dragging

time to the wood's slow sigh,
as she drops white crosses and Tanqueray,
racing her daddy to the finish line.

North Star

*Our present-day Polaris won't remain the North Star forever, due to
a motion of Earth known as the precession of the equinoxes.*
                              —Bruce McClure and Deborah Byrd,
                              "Gamma Cephei: A future Pole Star"

Evenings, we walked that path to barn and back,
me lagging behind as I navigated
cow patties and grassburs, Daddy never breaking
his stride. As his warm calloused hands swung
by his side, I'd reach up, land my hand in his,
feel its sure strength guide me back to the path.

Skipping in from school on days too cold
for plowing, I'd find his hands at work.
Newspapers spread around him, he shelled
pecans and kitchen warmth cocooned us
as I hummed to the steady *crack crack*
of the hulls. I watched his gloved hands shake
those pecans from the trees his father planted
on this land, trees I once thought would stand

forever, like the towering cliff behind
our house—oh, not really a cliff at all—
just sandstone outcropping, maybe five feet
tall. To my nine-year-old eyes that rock
seemed high as the sky, solid as a father,
but the fissure down its center foretold
how rain and cleaving roots would do their work,
and one day I found sandstone had let go,
left a fractured scrabble at my feet.

This morning, my father stumbles through
the kitchen in this house he built fifty years
ago as though he's tightrope walking
on a starless night. Trembling, he holds out
his hand. I clasp it tight, steadying his legs
for this journey across an unmapped stretch of sky.

Remembering His Name

My friend and I page through
his high school yearbook, the 1968
Blue Devil, giggling over bell bottoms
and bangs. Mostly, it's just what I expect:
his picture on every other page as cool
quarterback, president
of the senior class,
salutatorian. Inscriptions are scribbled
all over by fellow players and girls
with prom queen good looks.
Every message
is high school trite
until I come to one
from a boy named Gary,
which starts out usual
but ends with the truth:

You were lucky in high school
because people will remember
your name.

I ask about this one; my friend
says ten years after graduation,
Gary, doing eighty,
drove his car off a cliff.
Something about
that yearbook sentence
makes me want to find this boy,
whose picture appears
only once,
and tell him I understand
his black hunger
in driving over the edge,

hoping that years later
and miles from shattered glass,
someone would tell the story
to a woman, and she
would not forget his name.

Bobbie's Valediction

Valedictorian by default,
I knew I'd blow the speech: the honor
wasn't mine. I wanted to talk about
Bobbie, not yet twelve months in the grave,
but found myself sleep-walking down a road
of "the first day of the rest of our lives,"
a generic blue graduation gown
swallowing my gold-tasseled lies.

> *I remember her birthday*
> *was in February*
> *and she was scared*
> *sex might be messy*
>
> *I remember my letter*
> *waiting in her mailbox*
> *the day she died, how*
> *I confided the love bite*
>
> *on my neck from a summer*
> *crush, but said nothing*
> *of his hand down my pants,*
> *not wanting to leave her behind*

Some days I dream of a do-over
for that speech and think what I'd say:
how on the June afternoon her chestnut
gelding threw her, she'd left a list of things
to do: *clean room, apply for college*
scholarships, polish boots. Or maybe I'd read
Roethke's "Elegy for Jane," his student's
death so like Bobbie's own.

I'd find my way to honor Bobbie, finally,
by standing—speechless—on the stage, dead air
recalling for us all how she saddled up
and rode through the practice pasture, horse
and girl fluid dancers making perfect turns,
until the horse stumbled, missed the jump,
and Bobbie skimmed the clouds, hair floating
out in ribbons, contrails slicing the sky.

Freshman Composition

Cynthia turns her work in on time
all semester, though in October,
her mother slips into a coma
for two and a half essays, then dies.
I clip the obituary

and slide it into her hands the same
morning that LaShondra brings her baby
to class. The rest of us, homogeneous
and white, stumble over the baby's
name, Ejeeii. LaShondra repeats
it three times, like an incantation,

finally writes it on the board. The name
means "strong African warrior." He wakes
and I dance him around the room
in his Baby Gap sleeper and tiny
red Nikes, calm his cries by reviewing
comma splices. *Oh look, you've bored*

him back to sleep! We all laugh, but inside
I fear it's the one true comment
for the semester. Power-suited
in beige and black, once I was sure
I could make a difference, but as his mother
struggles over one more "C" paper,
one that will still lack

development and organization,
I wonder if I've cheated her
of early-morning lullabies
and given nothing she needs
in return. Or if Cynthia resents

hours spent on those first papers
while her mother's death hovered,
unexpected as a pop quiz.
And what of the other twenty-four
who've shared this bare, tiled room

for thirteen weeks? They write and write
while I, with my back turned,
scribble revision tips on the board,
a chalky scrawl erased
with the slam of a classroom door.

Hot Pink

Blue Beaumont dark reminds me I've flown
into unknown land, the thick, sweet heat
as foreign as the professional air
of this conference. Listening to discourse
on deconstructionist feminist criticism,

I worry over my poems, just my own words,
after all. What if someone shouts, *Throw this woman
out; she doesn't give a damn about deconstruction?*
But that's tomorrow. Tonight, someone pulls me

into a car and we head to Port Arthur
Mardi gras. Swallowed up in Cajun street songs,
I swig longnecks, sway among sequins. A girl
in a neon pink cat suit struts by, better than nude;

every man's head turns. I'm not even jealous, so perfect
is she poured into spandex second skin.
We follow her to the Fo'c's'le Bar
where the beer-bellied barkeep, waxing drunken,
throws Mardi gras beads. That girl and I jostle forward,

squealing, *Give us beads! We're whores
for beads!* The owner tosses cheap purple plastic
to her, then eyes me hard, and swirling
turquoise blesses the air, falls on my fingers,
a strand of perfect praise.

I learn the music of the street this night
and at next morning's meeting—my first
public reading—I lose my literary
virginity. Stripped bare, I give this crowd
what they want. Now, I am the hot pink girl

exposing more than sex. My words
undulate to the bump and grind
and I read for love: an amethyst strand
kissing my skin.

The Creative Writing Teacher Explains Love

You amble into class and settle down,
squeezing these 30-gallon trash bags
into the seats. Over the crackle
of plastic, I say write
and you go to it, opening your bags
and shaking out as much industrial grade
"love" and "pain" as possible
in fifteen minutes. Just once,

I want you to show me the rush
of love. Snuff it up your nose
and spit out the Sunday night
when you were fifteen and Emily Baker
bit your earlobe, leaving teeth marks
for a week. You told your mother
your dog, Chihuahua, did it. (Chihuahua,

that was the dog's name,
even though he was a pit bull—
tell me that, too). Your mother knew you were lying,
but did you care? No. That tiny chip
in Emily's left central incisor, secret nick
no one would notice except by touch, that ragged
sexiness was better than matching
Speidel I.D. bracelets. Tell me

everything. So you don't know
alliteration. Don't you love the sound
of *copper creel? Or Zaire and Zimbabwe?* Don't strand me
in a weatherless city; tell me the tropical zip code
of your affection.

Some Sunday night,
Emily will begin nibbling
again. That trash bag,
still in your lap, will open up,
gulp you both. Let me feel

her ridged teeth goosebumping
your neck. Let me hear
how you conjured a thousand lies
for your mother
as Emily's raspberry tongue slipped
out of your ear and lapped on down.

One July Night

After lovemaking
she steps into the light,
warm sperm spilling out
essence of babies
a ribbon down her legs.

Over 50 million
may be released
in a single burst,
she once read.
50 million emissaries
from his body to hers.
They don't stand a chance.

She wages war against them daily,
alters her body chemistry
so no two halves
ever join
in that feather quiet
docking of new soul
creation.

Seeming not to care,
they pursue this kamikaze
mission unaware
of her, the saboteur.
No babies are lovemade
this night.

Next to him once more, she wonders,
of those millions of cells,
bits of DNA and genetic codes,
which one has the recipe
for the burning blue in his eyes?

Does one bear the imprint
of his voice, instructions
for his wit?

She holds her breath,
trying to feel movement,
hoping to sense the reckless
abandonment
of forward propulsion.
She cannot.

But she smiles
as patterns of him
in intricate miniature
swim within her,
happy,
alive for hours.

Self-Composure

Caught in the half
world of sleep
undescended,
I begin
the silent recitation.

Stanzas slide
across my eyes,
words drop down,
clicking into place.
Prayer beads, loose
smooth pearls jostling
within the mother shell
before stringing.

Turn the words into necklaces
of prayer
strung across my breasts,
dripping thick
between shoulder blades,
running down my spine.

This is my midnight liturgy,
the only one left at this point
in the dark.
Say this poem first,
then the next,
remember why.
Whisper every word
and pray
those words will turn

water into wine
stone into bread
me into someone.

Some Electric Hum

for William Stafford and B.H. Fairchild

In barren Southwest Kansas, hardbaked edge
of the Great American Desert, natives
brag on empty air, a sky stretching out
for miles. What a shock to find instead
these heavy layers, a dense pentimento
streaked on sky's canvas waiting to be revised.

Stafford sensed it, too, wrote of touching rock
where Coronado walked, and that clanging armor
sways as Stafford's words hang on the breeze.
Fairchild later felt the charge of weighted air
as he roamed Liberal's streets, counting all doors
poems to be opened. Shop lathes sang to him

and play for me still. Some electric hum
lingers here, a multiplying pulse that sets us
down on the corner of Second and Main,
breathing in the same rearranged
molecules, just in different years.

The sky's so crowded with past vocabulary
that storm clouds spill verbs in the dirt, poetry
pooling underground in a space carved
out by a drained aquifer. Overhead,
stanzas glide on thermals, kite tails of iambs
and spondees shimmering in the heat.

This space masquerading as a mute Kansas stare
unfolds for me now an invitation
to grab hold, grapple with words just west
of the tongue. I catch the drift of remnants
as they eddy and roll, at last coalescing
into direction, a whisper on the wind: *Go.*

Notes

"Hammock Psalm" won second place in *Southwest Review's* 2017 Marr Poetry Prize competition.

"Sparks" was named a finalist in *Iron Horse Literary Review's* 2017 PhotoFinish Poetry Contest.

"The Promised Land" (under the title "Crossroads") was named a finalist in the 2017 Cultural Center of Cape Cod Poetry Contest

The group of poems, "Boys Would Come on Horses," "Breaking City Ordinances," "Remembering His Name" (under the title "Looking Through His Yearbook"), "Snake Trails," and "Coming Out of Rough Creek Canyon" was selected as the 1993 winner of the Texas Association of Creative Writing Teachers Student Poetry Award.

Read more at www.janicenortherns.com and follow her on Twitter @JaniceNortherns.